**IN A CITY
YOU WILL
NEVER VISIT**

IN A CITY
YOU WILL
NEVER VISIT

Young Smith

GreencupBooks

Copyright © Young Smith, 2017

ISBN: 978-1-943661-12-1

Originally published by California Institute of Arts and Letters (January 1, 2008).

Cover art by Jose Tonito

GreencupBooks
PO BOX 4945
Chattanooga, TN 37405
greencupbooks.com

CONTENTS

She Considers the Dimensions of Her Soul	1
The Properties of Light	3
Brief Discussion on His Body, Its Hands, and the Sun	4
The Properties of Light	6
Under the Powerline	7
The Properties of Light	9
What It Made Him Think of Was the Sea	11
Refluence	12
The Name of Her Illness	13
The Properties of Light	15
Woman Leaving the Land of Shinar	16
Inenarrabilis	18
There Were No Other Houses There for Miles	20
The Properties of Light	21
Big Bald Man	22
Rorqual	25
Translation of Ghalib (from No Original Text)	27
The Properties of Light	28
After the Rain	29
The Properties of Light	31
Prayer Concerning the Treachery of Her Hands	33
At a Diner Near the Airport	36

The Properties of Light	37
God's Instructions, Before His Visit	38
In a City You Will Never Visit	40
The Story of Watching	42
The Properties of Light	44
Small Couplets on One Passion of the Dead	45
Virus	46
The Properties of Light	48
Beneath the Waves	49
Squamata	50
The Properties of Light	51
Statue	52
The Properties of Light	53
The Serpent Imagines Another Version of Events	54
Poem Attempting to Deny the Body	56
The Properties of Light	57
What She Did on a Dark Night	58
My Achilles	59
The Properties of Light	62
She Was No Longer Hungry for Light	63
Canticle with Migratory Birds	65
Two Flowers	67
The Properties of Light	68
Lunar Isocolon (While Holding Her Breath)	69
About the Author	72

I

*The dark thing is hardly visible
in the leaves, under the sheen*

—Linda Gregg

SHE CONSIDERS THE DIMENSIONS OF HER SOUL

(Mrs. Morninghouse, after a Dreary Sermon Entitled, "What the Spirit Teaches Us through Grief")

The shape of her soul is a square.
She knows this to be the case
because she sometimes feels its corners
pressing sharp against the bone
just under her shoulder blades
and across the wings of her hips.
At one time, when she was younger,
she had hoped that it might be a cube,
but the years have worked to dispel
this illusion of space. So that now
she understands: it is a simple plane:
a shape with surface, but no volume—
a window without a building, an eye
without a mind.
                    Of course, this square
does not appear on x-rays, and often,
weeks may pass when she forgets
that it exists. When she does think
to consider its purpose in her life,
she can say only that it aches with
a single mystery for whose answer
she has long ago given up the search—
since that question is a name which can
never quite be asked. This yearning,
she has concluded, is the only function
of the square, repeated again and again
in each of its four matching angles,

until, with time, she is persuaded anew
to accept that what it frames has no
interest in ever making her happy.

THE PROPERTIES OF LIGHT

i. uncertainty principle

The light is an artichoke
built of glass,
whose bladed leaves,

at first, seem clear
and clean; yet as we
peel the bracts

that cup its heart,
each layer sheds
a smoky gleam,

revealing, to the patient
hand, scales of
unimagined shades—

hazel, auburn, almond,
bronze—until,
deep in its first

glossy flesh,
the light undresses
its darkness.

BRIEF DISCUSSION ON HIS BODY, ITS HANDS, AND THE SUN

(In Photographs of Her Late Husband, Mrs. Morninghouse Often Notices a Far-Away Look)

In the mirror he studied the hollows of its face,
the wrinkled purse of its scrotum, the bony knobs

of its wrists. Yet no matter which crease or joint
he examined, what he found were the lineaments

of another man's flesh. It seemed his duty,
however, to service its needs, so each morning

when it woke, he lathered its chin, plucked
the hairs from its nostrils, picked crust from its eyes.

He watched its fingers knot the tie at his collar,
then its legs, in his trousers, as they walked to his train.

Now and then, he heard it laugh or answer the questions
of others. As its tongue shaped the words, they sounded

borrowed and forced, and its opinions were rarely his own.
But he had learned not to challenge the humors of the body.

It was jealous of its rule and skilled at bringing pain.
He was, therefore, most often silent, lying coiled,

like an angleworm, beneath its ribs. He worried
now, though, that it might soon forget him.

While he made it a sandwich or washed its hair,
he felt like an echo, losing voice in the distance.

So late at night while it slept, he crouched in its ear.
"Be faithful," he whispered. "You won't live without me.

Without me you are nothing but a stone full of blood."
He tried to believe that his words found its conscience,

but to the body these commands were like the sifting
of the rain, only urging it more completely into silence,

where, while he waited for some twinge of concession,
it dreamed of its hands stirring the flames of the sun.

THE PROPERTIES OF LIGHT

ii. the beauty of the light

Light embraces the figure of a woman
      lying on a chair beneath

            a yellow lamp. When diffused, its rays
              begin to tumble

and spin, wrapping themselves about her
      shoulders and thighs.

            Scattered from their single course, its lines
              dissolve to a creamy film

of loops and scrolls and swirls—clinging,
      in a series of gentle

            gradations, from bright to dark, along her
              forearms and throat.

Much of what we call the beauty of light—
      like much of what we call

            the beauty of the body—is only the sum
              of this delicate confusion.

UNDER THE POWERLINE

What she works hardest to remember,
whenever she thinks of that Sunday morning,
is his face, there above the steering wheel,
watching the narrow road ahead as they wandered

out deep into the country, looking for a place
where they could finish being good together
at last. She could say that his hair was blonde,
lifting in the gusts through the open windows,

or that his eyes were blue, with a faint ring
of gold around the left iris, but the truth
is that these colors are little more than words
now, and that the faces she recalls when she lets

them out in the dark (as she often does, to hang
in the windows just before she sleeps), are never
the one she saw that morning, watching the road
between his hands as the hardtop failed to gravel,

then to a pair of ruts climbing through the hills.
Instead, what she sees are the better captured
smiles of Christmas cards and yellowed snapshots.
They are always pleasant faces, always handsome,

but, somehow, never quite his that morning,
when he stopped his father's car at the clearing's
edge and spit out his gum—never the eyes
that must have blinked too often, never the ear

she must have whispered to, never the mouth
that must have leaned close to answer: *Yes.
I'm sure. I do.* She could say that the clearing
was under a powerline, that he shook open a quilt

there on the grass, and that it was here that they lay
down among their scattered clothes, watching quietly
as, above them, the wind pushed the trees in circles
against the clouds. Yet these details are never firm:

Like those eyes in her windows late at night,
they drift and swell, then tumble out of frame,
and are soon lost. Like that clearing on the hill,
out there deep in the country, where the roads

unmapped themselves—where she could say they
were once, for a few hours, on a quilt beside a car,
but where, even then, she suspected what it would
become: a place she has been leaving ever since.

THE PROPERTIES OF LIGHT

iii. c

At the speed of light,
there is no passage of time.
There are photons, then,

created at the instant
the universe was born

that have not aged
a moment since.

However far this light
has traveled, crossing
whatever great tracts

of darkness, it exists
in a state of ceaseless

beginning, never finding
a way to the edge

of its future, never
leaving the ancient
frontier of its past:

Pity the old light
this endless birth.

Give thanks each evening
for the sorrows of dusk.

WHAT IT MADE HIM THINK OF WAS THE SEA

(Mrs. Morninghouse Overhears a Policeman Describe the Curious Scene of Her Husband's Death)

We found him in a room at the Westway Inn,
one of those airport motels with the tall
wooden fences to hide adulterers' cars.
His nude body in a chair by the dresser,
the revolver on the floor between his feet.
He'd left the shower running while he did it,
with his shoes and clothes soaking in the tub.
There was no note or wallet, no keys,
no car outside, no one who'd heard the shot.
While we waited for the photographer,
my partner pointed across the street,
above the rows of bad-credit car lots,
at the tinsel streamers rolling in the breeze.
He said what it made him think of was the sea.

REFLUENCE

(Mrs. Morninghouse Resents the Interference of the Moon)

Tonight, on our side of the planet,
the moon lifts the sea to a bulge near its center, drawing the waters
away from our shores. Meanwhile,

some eight thousand miles beneath us,
the gravity of the moon reaches down through the earth, pulling
the sea to a trough near its center,

then pressing its waters—through the force
of displacement—up the sands of those other distant coasts.
In this way, the moon confounds

our longing for stillness, demanding
that we share—each night, with these unresting currents—
the burden of its solitary mass.

THE NAME OF HER ILLNESS

(Mrs. Morninghouse Disagrees with the Psychiatrist's Diagnosis)

No, the name of her illness

is impossible to pronounce,

though for hours each night

the word rakes through her bones.

Deep in her limbs, in the spongy

marrow of her skull,

its consonants thrust

at the curves of its vowels,

their ascenders and serifs

like the teeth of a saw—

shearing the cartilage

that binds her together

until she lies, hardly breathing,

in a stranger's loose flesh.

If only once she could say it—

if just once its syllables

would part on her tongue—

then, she is sure,

she would spoil its power:

With one brush of her voice,

the name would open

and fall.

THE PROPERTIES OF LIGHT

iv. the light in d minor

The sun poured out its golden rhythm:
Its light was a music of double bass and tenoroons.

That music fell down on the roofs of our churches, and soon
the roofs of our churches were the bronze of its gongs.

The gargoyles and chimney-pots throbbed with its motions.
The sun was a drummer with parturient wrists.

It hammered its beams to the voices of choirs,
bursting the time of their angular psalms,

tangled its fire in the great pipes of the organs,
shook open the skirts of the prayermasters' gowns.

The bell towers groaned beneath this ruckus of marvels
while their steeples, like fingers, brushed at the sky.

Until the sun, when it saw how the faithful were cowering—
though it wanted no fear for the life it would give—

turned away from those timid rites at the altars,
silenced its blessings, and dulled its bold eye.

WOMAN LEAVING THE LAND OF SHINAR

And the LORD said, Behold, the people is one, and they have all one language; and this they begin to do: and now nothing will be restrained from them, which they have imagined to do.

What was it we imagined to do?
I can't recall now, honestly,

not since this terrible noise began,
falling in strokes among the tents.

Here is the tower, and beneath it,
the stacks of bricks, the smoking kilns,

and yet—why should we build a tower
here, on this bare and windy plain?

What was it we hoped to find there,
above the trees, among the clouds?

There is no one left to ask. All the voices
of my neighbors are like the speech

of birds. Even my children no longer
answer to my calls. Like the rest,

they only bleat and growl in strangled
tongues. Their cries might be the shiver

of prayers, or the howls of curses—
I can't tell which.

The men tear at their beards,
and the women twist their hands,

as if only their fingers could describe
the shape of their sorrows.

Here, no words will fasten to the dark.
No ear will meet the stories we must tell.

I will go, then, and speak with the waters
of the river, as I see the others, setting out

to speak with the mountains or the stars.
It is only there now, we know, scattered

abroad upon the face of the earth,
far from the shadows of these walls

which had seemed home, that any one of us
can hope to make ourselves a name.

INENARRABILIS

Raining April afternoon, a small park in the city, voices moving
on wet stone. At first, the cold air lifts and scatters the sound,

confusing its direction. Like the rain, it is everywhere,
and I move through it, along the paths of flowers, until I find

the source: five women kneeling at the edge of a fountain,
hands clasped in a circle, foreheads touching the pavement

as their cries spill up from the water—first, a deep moaning,
then a hoarse push of consonants: not quite language yet,

and not quite song—though full of urgent music.
The women shudder, lost in their prayers, while an old man

with a Bible leans over their backs. When he calls, the women
answer with new tangles of sound, lifting their arms above

their heads in trembling gestures of flight. Near the fountain,
they gather stares as others join me to watch. When our eyes meet,

we are quick to confirm our own good sense, to deny
any fellowship with these coarse women on the ground,

whose faces are screened under wet curtains of hair as the wild
noise moves among them. They feel our judgments, I can tell,

but welcome our ridicule. It is what they have come for,
why they are here. With the damp air, they breathe it in,

then give it back in shouts, their voices climbing as they work
to heal us of our sad contempt. While they keen and sough,

the old man walks among us, searching our faces for some sign
of Glory at work, but as he comes near, we look away, unwilling

to meet the rude mercy in his eyes—yet he isn't disappointed.
For him, the offer is enough. All that his plain God requires.

When we step back, refusing his hand, he nods, then leaves us
for the women at the fountain, back to the clean grace of water

falling on water, where he smiles as he listens to the wet bursts
of their praises—filled with what we refuse, hearing what we won't.

THERE WERE NO OTHER HOUSES THERE FOR MILES

(Mrs. Morninghouse, on a Silent Trip with Her Husband, Several Weeks before His Death)

It was late at night on an winding road
when they topped the hill and saw the trailer
burning in the middle of a field—flames
rolling blue in its broken windows, heat
shaking the trees above its roof in wide
circles against an orange wall of smoke.
There were no other houses there for miles,
only the long gravel driveway leading up
to a swingset and a motorcycle parked
at the foot of the cinderblock steps.
                    "Don't," he said when she
touched the brake, and so they didn't stop.
The next afternoon, while they ate lunch
in a diner several counties north,
she was careful not to read the papers.

THE PROPERTIES OF LIGHT

v. the illusion of local causes is undone

The light collects its names from the lips of children
while they sleep, eager for the dawn and the coming

glories of the sun. On such lips there are many names,
but each is lovely to the light: the tender words

of tender souls who live by rules of kindness, even
in their sleep—and once the light has torn those names

from the hush of dreaming mouths, it makes of them
its shadows on the walls of burning houses.

BIG BALD MAN

(Mrs. Morninghouse Looks at a Painting She Bought with Her Husband Years Ago)

We found him at a moving sale on a street
down near the river, leaning on a chair

in a little shotgun house—a wide bald head,
oil on fiberboard, without a frame, his face

a white moon the size of a wheelbarrow.
The painter was leaving the city—

right away, she said—so was anxious to empty
the place. While we admired his pink shoulders

and his troweled eyes, she wouldn't meet
his dusty look there in the corner.

She was finished, I could tell, giving up
on a life she had hoped would carry her.

She took our first offer—forty dollars—
and her big bald man was ours.

He has lived with us ever since, moving
from house to house, hung from the nails

we drove in our landlords' studs. While it's true
that, lately, I don't often see him anymore—

above the dining table, behind the ironing
board, between a pair of hanging plants—

most days, he doesn't appear to mind.
He fills whatever wall I give him

and never looks to suffer. Though there are
some nights, when I'm up late drinking wine,

when I can feel him dreaming of that first
narrow house—of the easel's quiet tilt,

of the woman's hands stirring the pigments,
pulling the hairs of the brush to mold

his jaw. He can hear her footsteps
on the dropcloth, smell the gesso

and the linseed as he recalls those hours
of wet new life, his eyes gathering

shape in hers, her fingers filling his ears
with their first strange sounds of ships' horns

from the river, her quick breath warming
his face until the drying fixed his stare,

leaving him—finshed and still—with only
her brief faith to remember.

RORQUAL

(Mrs. Morninghouse Watches a Documentary at the Museum of Natural Science)

As the film explains, the blue whale's heart
is the size of a small Japanese sedan.
Children, if he allowed it, could crawl

through his major arteries. A man might
build a small hut on the flukes of his tail.
And yet, on the screen, his pale eye shows

no awareness of its body's might. He lives
to move, leaves all the staring to the camera
as—beneath the helicopter—his great sulfur

belly pulls through the red drifts of krill.
While we listen to the deep work of his lungs—
the sounding moans, the breaching sighs—

the narrator details what little we know
about the secret course of his migrations,
how he makes those long journeys alone,

without our eyes to follow, from the wide
plankton meadows at the green equator
to the bright puzzles of ice at the pole:

No wonder the old need to spear his flesh.
I feel it again, rising up warm now in this quiet
room, where we watch him leap and roll

among the swells. And I won't deny it: the urge
to lift the dart, to feel the iron splitting bone,
the tarred hemp scraping on the gunwales

as the monster drags us out to some dark new
climate, where—under unfamiliar stars, at last—
we smite that heart and claim our unruly dominion.

TRANSLATION OF GHALIB (FROM NO ORIGINAL TEXT)

(Mrs. Morninghouse Finds Little Comfort in Her Husband's Favorite Writer)

I waited for you there, in a damp arbor near the ocean; the wind made voices among the rooms of vines, but none of them was yours.

I burned green twigs and flowers on a stone above the waves; I spoke the beckoning words, but found no guiding shapes within the smoke.

I watched the sea for your coming, let my mind walk to meet you over its great rafts of kelp, but the waters told me nothing of your will.

The sun was a dying circle in the fog above the coast; my prayers descended with its flames, until they wore a hood of dusk.

My welcome lost, at last, among the fragrant shadows of the leaves, I had only the husks of words to gather for my desire.

THE PROPERTIES OF LIGHT

vi. an augury of the light

What we observe is not nature itself, but nature exposed to our method of questioning.
                              —Werner Heisenberg

In the laboratories
the instruments perform
the stark haruspicy
of light, divining—
from its dismembered
beams—only the narrow
weathers of the eye.

AFTER THE RAIN

Of course, no one believed him when he told us about the storm.
And God said, the end of all flesh is come before me...

Seriously, now—what would you have thought? So as we watched
him there on the hilltop, hewing the gopher wood, pacing off the cubits,

we jeered at his sons and their meek little wives, and we laughed
at his big ungainly boat while the clouds gathered tall overhead.

He was wrong, it seems, only in degree. Some of us would survive
(you'd be astonished by the number of things that will float),

and yet, for each of us who lived, there were dozens drowned:
We lost three sons ourselves, and my husband's youngest bride—

a girl of twelve with dark eyes and a doll made of twigs
in her pocket, who called to me, again and again, between

the great cracks of thunder—"Mother! Old Mother, please!"—
until the water gripped her shoulders, then swallowed her hair.

You'll understand, then, why these days, whenever I see some wild
fellow yanking at his beard, or twitching his bony fingers at the sky,

I gather my remaining loved ones close. After all, if I am sure of nothing
else now, it is that I am not the sort of woman this God will talk to,

and that if I hope to keep my children with me in His strange and wicked world, I must learn to trust the promises of fools.

THE PROPERTIES OF LIGHT

vii. the many worlds interpretation

A quasar,
so the musing
physicists suggest,

is a siphon
breathing light
from another

universe beyond
the distant borders
of our own.

Just as black holes
are also siphons,
breathing light

from our own stars
to burst as quasars
in other distant

realms. Therefore,
it seems, the *causa
causans* is a mind

whose fiery
thoughts unseal
the sky. Whose

desires, like its
dimensions, can
bear no human

scale or story—whose
musing only light
itself describes.

PRAYER CONCERNING THE TREACHERY OF HER HANDS

(In Her Reflection, Mrs. Morninghouse Begins to See a Familiar Far-Away Look)

Take my hands, please Lord,
and give me another pair.

These I have can no longer be trusted.
They are deceitful hands. Cunning hands.
Hands with no proper sense of duty or shame.

Drawers and trunks, no matter whose, are theirs to open.
No matter the risk to me, others' cabinets are theirs to explore.

Every day now I worry what they might do next.
At concerts, I must clamp them tight between my legs,
resisting their urge to applaud between movements.

In museums, they long to stroke the thighs of statues.
In magazines, they rub photographs of jewels and German cars.

What does this say of their character?
To my hands, Lord, this is a childish question.

They are too pleased with themselves.
Too convinced of their value.
Too certain that I will excuse their faults.

For a time long ago, several of the fingers were honest.
They pointed at the stars.
They sketched the faces of children.

They ached deep in their knuckles
at the cruelty of the world.

But in a few years, their nature was poisoned
by the others. Their goodness made them weak,
and soon they were as wicked as the rest—

never truly themselves any longer
unless counting money or tying knots.

I have tried, Lord, I have, to lead them
back to virtue, but even in the garden, tending
flowers, their gestures are shadowed with contempt.

They have begun, I can tell, a quiet strategy of revolt.
Their method is shrewd, but I sense its meaning
 in the way they shuffle cards or fasten buttons—

they intend to free themselves entirely
from the service of my will.

Be assured, Lord, I resist them.
I have stung them with nettles,
thrust them into icy water,

held them trembling over the red eyes
of stoves—but still they refuse to submit.

They have grown far too fond
of sharpening knives, of crushing ants
with their nails, of striking matches.

Before I know what they're up to
they have slipped from my pockets,

and I soon wake to find them writing
curses in hymnals, or touching
the hair of strangers on a bus.

This is why you must hear me, Lord,
and take them quickly. Far more than mine
now, these hands are *Your* creatures,

and I will not be judged myself
for the dark things they hope to do.

AT A DINER NEAR THE AIRPORT

(Mrs. Morninghouse Hears a Story about Her Husband's Final Meal)

When he took a stool near my own at the counter,
he looked to me like a man who had forgotten

how to sleep, with broken eyes behind his glasses.
He ordered a pie, and the waitress asked what flavor.

He said he didn't care, but when she cut a wedge
of chocolate, he sighed and squeezed his temples.

"No," he said. "I came here to eat a pie, and that's exactly
what I mean to do." The waitress glanced my way.

She tapped her pad, and when I shrugged, she shrugged,
then brought the man the pie. "Lemon," she whispered—to me.

We shared an ashtray while we watched him eat it from the tin,
chewing slowly, with his eyes shut. When the pie was gone,

he paid his check and wiped his fingers on his shirt. "There,"
he said—and this was all he said—"That should do it."

THE PROPERTIES OF LIGHT

viii. two conversations with the light

Here is an early conversation
with the light:

a girl on a hilltop
throwing rocks
at the sun.

And here is a much later conversation
with the light:

a woman on a hilltop
throwing her name
at the sun.

GOD'S INSTRUCTIONS, BEFORE HIS VISIT

When I come, don't ask me those questions you know I never
 answer.
Instead, offer me a cigarette and a cup of warm rum.

A chair near the window. A quilt for my legs.
When I sleep, draw the blinds. Fold my hands in my lap.

Keep the flies and the nervous dead away.
If I stir while I dream, whisper my name softly.

Brush my hair with your fingers and sing to me—
something sweet and childish and slow.

Make me young with your voice, for a few hours,
until I find the strength again to love you.

When I wake, let me leave quietly.
Don't trouble me with prayers you know I won't remember.

Instead, tie my shoes. Button my collar.
Hold the door and take my hand on the stairs.

Say nothing when we part.
Only kiss me gently on the forehead.

Point me to the road
that will lead me home.

II

I am who I am
oh lord cold as the thoughts of birds

—W.S. Merwin

IN A CITY YOU WILL NEVER VISIT

(Mrs. Morninghouse Rejects Her Doctors' Advice to Travel)

Tonight, in a city you will never visit,
no one finds your absence strange.

In that Kitchener or Jabalpur,
that Shadrinsk or P'yongyang,

no one waits for you to call,
no one expects you at a party,

no one searches for your face
among a crowd of passersby.

If an alto sings off key somewhere
in that Yerevan or Belomorsk,

that Gwangju or Kinshasa,
no one is reminded of your voice.

You are the subject of no rumors,
whether counterfeit or true,

in that Riga or that Reykjavik,
that Kursk or Saskatoon,

and in that Aberdeen or Abidjan,
that Taipei or Bucharest,

no one envies your good fortune
or begrudges your old debts

(just as no one grits his teeth there
at the mention of your name

or relives a dark embarrassment
for which you were to blame).

We'll find your eyes in no one's dreams,
then, in that Banjul or Jacarta,

no one listening for your footsteps
in that Woollahra or Dakar,

and in the morning when you don't
appear, no one will be surprised,

since those who might have hoped
you'd come will not yet have arrived.

THE STORY OF WATCHING

*It is a primitive form of thought that
either things exist or do not exist.*
                    —Sir Arthur Eddington

Our thoughts are objects, made of matter's stuff,
in their germ, no less solid than iron or stone.

As such, a room remembered is itself a room,
whose windows are not apparitions,

but squares of earnest glass. Whose door
is not an eidolon, but a passage

to another space, yet to be assembled.
The reverse is true as well:

Whatever it seems we should believe,
those floors we trust as wood or marble,

whose weight and presence our feet confirm,
are thoughts themselves, made of notion's fabric,

no more solid at their winking source
than imagined windows or remembered doors.

We live among these rooms we build—
of brick or thinking, of now or then—

where the walls are a voice in the story of watching,
trembling to speak their shelter in our touch.

THE PROPERTIES OF LIGHT

ix. light considered in the role of belligerent

These are the allies
of the light:

anemones
marmosets
gods carved from stone
dragonflies
hoarfrost
the bells of trombones
checkerboards
jellyfish
the craters of Neptune
howitzers
monstrances
patent leather shoes

These are the enemies
of the light:

foghorns
photographs
radial symmetry
prisms
parentheses
the false glow of dreams
yashmaks
stopwatches
heliostats
firefighters
parasols
requiescats

SMALL COUPLETS ON ONE PASSION OF THE DEAD

Late at night the dead come
to admire our bodies.

With slow fingers they discover
each blade of our ribs,

each seam of our tendons,
each groove of our spines.

Kneeling for hours beside
our beds, they touch our

moles, our birthmarks,
our wrinkles, our scars.

They trace the curves of our noses.
They count the fillings in our teeth.

The dead are careful not to wake us.
They have no desire for conversation.

They are slightly ashamed
to be in our rooms at all.

Yet they can't turn away.
Our beauty confounds them

while they watch the blood move
the veins on the backs of our hands.

VIRUS

(Mrs. Morninghouse Discovers One of the Disappointments of Getting Well)

How it begins
the delicate

curling into fever
thoughts losing

surface dreams
narrowed to scattered

lights aware only
of the wet ache

of a molar
in the jaw

the distant throb
of a toe-knuckle

an eyelash burning
in its pore

While it lasts
a not altogether

unwelcome reprieve
of destination

hot quiet
of the blood

whispering through
each polished cell

until the virus
loses strength

until the windows
start to firm

until that bright
absence leaves

and the faces
in the dresser

photographs
gather names.

THE PROPERTIES OF LIGHT

x. collapse of the wave function

Like you, the light
that warms your papery
brow would prefer
very much not to die—

or, since death is its lot
as much as yours—
to die, at least, in some
more handsome spot.

BENEATH THE WAVES

(Mrs. Morninghouse Welcomes a New Understanding of the Sea)

On the bus one evening, she met a fat little man
with a face full of warts where his beard should have been.
He was interested in the mysteries of deep ocean vents,

where, he said, there are life forms found nowhere else
on the planet. Great clusters of tube worms, for example,
waving in the dark—many of them over six feet in length!

You could find pale spider crabs there and giant white clams,
carpets of starfish, clouds of blind shrimp. Until recently,
he said, before the lamps of the submarines found their way

at last to those fields of chimneys, not a single photon of light
had ever brushed the black trenches where they lay.
The little man showed her photographs in a large book

on the subject, and as she studied his pictures, she came to see how,
as he put it, alone in bed late at night, one might find a peculiar
comfort in this landscape with no use for eyes.

SQUAMATA

Draped on the lens of the gas meter's dial,
the golden lizard declares her form.

She makes a ripeness where she stands,
a burl of luster among the raddled ferns.

Spathe of copper, breathing thorn
of brass, her stillness is a climate

of its own—a deed of presence only—
and all the morning is a captive of her work.

THE PROPERTIES OF LIGHT

xi. a consolation of the light

Through the varnished gloss of noon, a widow with a briefcase climbs to the top of a mountain. There, sitting on a tree stump, she opens the briefcase in her lap. Inside are several large specimens of chalcedony—jasper, chrysoprase, carnelian. These she lifts in turn to her eye, inspecting the sun through the broken faces of the stones, until, as their quiet shadows pool across her brow—first green, then red, then green again—she comes to know the several mercies of translucence.

STATUE

The statue is weighted with the eyes of all
        those who have ever come to look at it.

Over the years, their gazes have collected
        on its surface, until what stands before us

is made less of stone than of this residue
        of sight. So that today the boy who climbs

on the statue does not climb on marble,
        so much as on the witness of these others

who have dressed it with their stares—and those,
        like myself, here watching the child, will soon

clothe it with him as well. So that the statue we
        have made will always be one with a boy

on its shoulders, pulling at its ears and shouting,
        "Wake up, sir! Sir, wake up!"

THE PROPERTIES OF LIGHT

xii. iridial

As she walks from the bathtub to the kitchen
for one of the towels folded there on the ironing board,

the sun drops below the eaves of the west-facing windows,
filling the room with a soft amber flush—while behind her,

on the tile just outside the bathroom door,
the cat drinks from one of her golden footprints.

THE SERPENT IMAGINES ANOTHER VERSION OF EVENTS

When the woman approached the tree of the Knowledge of Good
    and Evil,
I lay waiting there, just as it was written, in the grass.

Yet when I gazed upon her eyes, the look I discovered made me
    pause.
It was too clear there in her face, how—without knowing it herself—
    she longed
to taste of the fruit of the tree, just as she longed to hear those words

that, from the start, my cloven tongue had been shaped to speak:
And your eyes shall be opened, and ye shall be as gods...

Though all my creeping flesh urged me to say these things so long
rehearsed within my blood, still, I was a subtle creature by design,
and when I understood the roles the tale would ask us both to play,

I smiled my narrow serpent's smile and chose another story.
Without a word, then, I climbed the tree and ate its fruit myself,

winding darkly through the branches until each limb was freed of
    weight.
When this was done, and I was well-full of that hard wisdom bred
    for the soul
of man, I bore deep into the earth and strangled the tree by its roots.

Later, in the cool of the day, when the woman and the man heard
    the voice
of the Lord God walking in the garden, they were not afraid. Neither
    did

they hide themselves, so that when He found them, they were
    lying naked
on the grass, eating, from my basket, the fruits of the Tree of
    Life.
Seeing this, the Lord God was perplexed. The words He had made
    to speak

no longer fit the scene. There would be, He knew, no sorrows
    now to multiply,
nor any cause to bring forth thorns and thistles from the field. The
    woman

would bear no offspring to favor or to shun; the man would eat
    no bread
in the sweat of his face, nor would he ever return now to the
    earth from which
he was made. I smiled once more as I watched my Maker grieve
    upon the sight,

and by that smile, the Lord saw all that had happened in His
    absence.
As we had both known that He must, the Lord God cursed me
    then,

so that I should go always on my belly, and eat of the dust all the
    days of my life—
though there was little joy now in His work, as there was only joy
    left in the story.
Since that day, with the Cherubims' sword across his lap, the Lord
    sits on a stone

just outside the garden gates, where with His angels, He watches
    His children dancing
in an endless noon—without shame, without beauty—around my
    ruined tree.

POEM ATTEMPTING TO DENY THE BODY

(Mrs Morninghouse Grows Weary of Taking Her Medication)

Every poem is about the body—except this one.
This poem refuses the language of the flesh.

If you strike this poem, it will not bruise.
If you embrace its narrow lines, however

tenderly, it will find no comfort in your touch.
Put an ear to one of its stanzas: you will detect

no respiration (even if its rhythms sometimes
duplicate the action of a heart). Above all,

this poem resents the tyranny of the image,
and is most pleased with itself when most

odorless and pale. It craves the poise
of a theorem, the dignity of a law; it aspires

to a state of perfect abstraction. Dear reader,
please, allow my little poem what it desires:

Let it trust, however tenderly, its hope
that it may live without your voice.

THE PROPERTIES OF LIGHT

xiii. the light as a silky motion in the constellation of
—Centaurus

Alone in her Peruvian mountain retreat,
the aged astronomer sits on her laddered seat,

bent toward the heavens like an heliotrope
at the end of her twelve-foot telescope,

pulling the music that wrinkles just under her skin
from the white hairs on her aged Hegelian chin.

The astronomer has not lost her mind—
she has given it away to the stars—

and each evening at the lens of her twelve-foot eye,
she charts its journeys across the Southern sky:

another child of the brilliant Peruvian night,
waltzing in a robe of young Peruvian light.

WHAT SHE DID ON A DARK NIGHT

(Mrs. Morninghouse Full of Wine, after Reading Again a Favorite Poem by Ms. Swenson)

Unsnapped the stays of the stars' bright girdle.

Plucked chords on vines and slender saplings' trunks.

Kneeled among cypress knees, scratched wings with locusts.

Combed a part in the wet ferns on a balding mountain's scalp.

Grubbed with centipedes through the pulp of rot-softened stumps.

Brooded with lichen in the dripping belfries of caves.

Carved noses on boulders with the sandy wind of her voice.

Turned birch leaves to drumskins, spruce needles to dim-gleaming wicks.

Swayed with a shiver of moon high in the cloud-dampened timber.

Vanished—as gods will—in the first pink of dawn.

MY ACHILLES

(A Heroine for Mrs. Morninghouse)

I think of you always
there in the court
of Lycomedes,

where your mother—
sorrowing nymph—
hoped to hide you

as a girl from the fate
of heroes; not yet
the key to the poet's

vaulting design, still
a thing of jewels
and gossip, a gleaming

ornament, like the rest—
one of those
drowsy virgins

scattered on the rugs,
spinning flax,
plaiting garlands,

dressing the urns
with sprigs of crocus
and vetch.

Soon enough, of course,
the plot—the noise of bronze,
the steam of corpse fires...

And yet always
in my version
of events,

you never leave
Scyros; Odysseus
never solves

your mother's ruse,
so that even now
you are there,

combing wool
on the floor
among that white

company of maidens,
your hair damp
with rosewater,

your eyes veiled
with muslin,
your slender arms

bright with the oil
of bergamot
and myrrh—

forever something
whispered, something
lyric and small—

forever one
of those sashed
and lovely women,

sighing on the rugs,
whose stories were never
cruel enough to tell.

THE PROPERTIES OF LIGHT

xiv. description of a pear on a pewter dish

But pears prove to be impossible to describe.
     —Czeslaw Milosz
      on Stevens' "Study of
      Two Pears"

See the blue there shadowed
beneath the yellow's gloss.

That blue is the sky
within the cutis of the pear.

At night this sky grows dark
and unfolds a crust of distant stars:

It is these pale fires within its skin
that give the pear its taste of heaven.

SHE WAS NO LONGER HUNGRY FOR LIGHT

(Mrs. Morninghouse Swallows a Star)

She had long hoped to meet the eyes of God
in the vast furnace of a star, but when, that night,
she pulled one from the vault of the moonless sky,

it was, she found, no larger than a single
grain of salt. It did not burn her fingers.
Instead, its fires were cold, and left a pinch,

like winter rain, across her lips. The flavor
was not at all what one would expect.
There was no burst of plentitude, no rush

of shoreless wisdom past all reach of human
thought. It traveled silently through her throat
and stomach, until it dissolved into a thousand

tiny flames and met her blood. What did she
become, then, with those flakes of broken
incandescence pressing in her veins?

Nothing at all that one might expect.
She was not lifted from her chair to swim
among the clouds. There were no sighs

of angels to haunt her skull—no jolts of cosmic
bristling in her cells. Instead, it seemed the task
of each spark to urge her toward her bed,

and there, soon afterwards, for three days
and nights, she vanished into sleep.
When she awoke, the house was dark.

She walked outside and found a sky cauled
with the milk of the northern stars—and though
again she raised her hands, she was no longer

hungry for light. Instead, she let her fingers
drift through the black fields between each
shivering point—since it was there, the star

had taught her—with its three days of silent,
ice-stung dreams—that she must learn to live
if she would know the lives of the heavens.

CANTICLE WITH MIGRATORY BIRDS

Let her mind be a gourd hanging
from a backyard pole, and let the martin

come there to make its summer visit.
Let it plait young twigs with leaves

and mud in the hollow of her brow
and groom its purple feathers
under the shelter of her regard.

Give the bird a mate and a brood
of hatchlings to share its tufted nest,

and while they idle here among
the languid gardens of her will,

let them adorn her conceits
with the jeweled husks of insects,
with broomstraw and cornsilk

gathered from the wind.
Let this craft be her only return

for their keeping—a fretwork
of notions wound with thistle

and floss—and when the birds
have departed, making south
for the green shadows of Brazil,

let these forms remain as a vessel
to preserve her thoughts of June.

In days of snow and narrow light,
let her bring the gourd down

from its pole: Let her shake it gently
and hear inside the dry brush
of a wreath across its shell.

TWO FLOWERS

(Mrs. Morninghouse, at Dusk, in Her Husband's Garden)

The white orchid blooms and gives its dampness,
gives the loose shadows of its petals, gives its sheen,
its beaded stem, the reaching softness of its clutch.

Her mind is a flower as well, no longer circumscribed
by thought—she breathes as the orchid breathes,
and lends her watching to its shapes.

With the white flower of her mind, she makes
the pooling shadows on the soil, the dripping stem,
the opal sheen, the weightless fingers of the petals.

She gives as the orchid gives, reaching softly
in wet shadows—another gentle pulse of evening
in this white garden safe from thought.

THE PROPERTIES OF LIGHT

xv. illuminance

Beneath the aureole
always the umbra—

that "blackest region
of a shadow"—

though beneath
the umbra, as beneath

the cysted flocculi
of the sun, always

a deeper light
that gives the dark

its burnish—and it is
in this subtle gleaming

of the black,
in this quiet *here*

beneath the absence,
that the light achieves

its first and only
deliverance from grief.

LUNAR ISOCOLON (WHILE HOLDING HER BREATH)

(Mrs. Morninghouse Resolves Her Disagreements with the Moon)

The moon is an eye that never opens.
It is the shell of a mollusk.
It is the head of a match.

The moon is a bladder full of yellow milk,
whose skin, at any moment, may be
burst by the needles of the pines.

The moon is a coin of a small
African nation, crossing a mirror
in a young girl's room.

The moon is the stone of an apricot.
It is the bulb of a tulip
It is the ash of a cigar.

The moon is the spiracle
of a breaching porpoise.
It is a grain of barley,

and it is the scar of a pox.
It is a cyst, a saucer, a cervix
of tin, a coil of burning

tungsten, a communion wafer.
The moon is the head of Orpheus
singing among the waves.

The moon is each of these things
not in turn, but at once, for the woman
who lies on the floor of a pond,

looking up through the golden mouth
in its surface—where a dragonfly
stands on the face of the moon.

Where the moon is, at last, a woman's eye
under water—dark with the shadows
of craters, splintered by wings of glass.

ABOUT THE AUTHOR

Young Smith has received fellowships from the National Endowment for the Arts, the James A. Michener foundation, and the Kennedy Arts Council, as well as a Tennessee Williams Scholarship from the Sewanee Writer's Conference. His poems have appeared in many journals. He is an associate professor of English at Eastern Kentucky University. He lives with his wife, Janet Schwartz, and their daughter, Harper, in Lexington, Kentucky.

www.ingramcontent.com/pod-product-compliance
Lightning Source LLC
Chambersburg PA
CBHW021449080526
44588CB00009B/760